DOVER · THRIFT · EDITIONS

Poems of Solace and Remembrance

Edited by

PAUL NEGRI

DOVER PUBLICATIONS, INC.
Mineola, New York

DOVER THRIFT EDITIONS

GENERAL EDITOR: PAUL NEGRI

❧

Dedicated in loving memory to
Hayward Cirker

I can not say, and I will not say,
That he is dead—he is just away.

—James Whitcomb Riley

Copyright

Bibliographical Note

Poems of Solace and Remembrance is a new work, first published by Dover Publications, Inc., in 2001.

International Standard Book Number

ISBN-13: 978-0-486-41584-0
ISBN-10: 0-486-41584-8

Manufactured in the United States by Courier Corporation
41584802 2014
www.doverpublications.com

Note

Give sorrow words; the grief that does not speak
Whispers the o'er-fraught heart and bids it break.
Shakespeare, *Macbeth*

Poets over the centuries have strived to give sorrow words and permit grief to speak in multifarious voices. Those suffering bereavement, loss, or travail have often found solace and comfort in sharing the feelings of others who have expressed their sorrow, love, faith, and remembrance in memorable verse.

The poems in this concise volume span four centuries and display a rich variety of styles and sensibilities, from Walter Raleigh's calm acceptance in "Even Such Is Time" to Dylan Thomas's passionate defiance in "Do Not Go Gentle into That Good Night." Included are works by such great English and American poets as Shakespeare, Wordsworth, Dickinson, Whitman, Christina Rossetti, and Robert Frost, as well as poems by writers whose names are now generally forgotten, but who have struck in their verses the resonant chord common to the hearts of all who have suffered loss or contemplated the end of life.

Whether read aloud at memorial services or read silently for personal inspiration, may these poems offer to all some measure of solace and the assurance that no one grieves alone.

Acknowledgments

W. H. Auden: "Funeral Blues" from *W. H. Auden Collected Poems* by W. H. Auden. Copyright © 1940 & renewed 1968 by W. H. Auden. Reprinted by permission of Random House, Inc. and Faber and Faber Ltd.

Robert Frost: "Acceptance" from *The Poetry of Robert Frost* edited by Edward Connery Lathem, the Estate of Robert Frost and Jonathan Cape as publisher. Copyright © 1928, 1969 by Henry Holt and Co. © 1956 by Robert Frost. Reprinted by permission of Henry Holt and Company, LLC and The Random House Group Limited.

Edna St. Vincent Millay: "Dirge Without Music" by Edna St. Vincent Millay. From *Collected Poems*, HarperCollins. Copyright © 1928, 1955 by Edna St. Vincent Millay and Norma Millay Ellis. All rights reserved. Reprinted by permission of Elizabeth Barnett, literary executor.

John Masefield: "A Song at Parting" from *The Poems and Plays of John Masefield* by John Masefield. Reprinted by permission of The Society of Authors as the Literary Representative of the Estate of John Masefield.

Dylan Thomas: "Do Not Go Gentle into That Good Night" from *The Poems of Dylan Thomas*. Copyright © 1952 by Dylan Thomas. Reprinted by permission of New Directions Publishing Corp. and David Higham Associates.

Contents

PAGE

King James Bible
Psalm 23 (The Lord is my shepherd) 1
Walter Raleigh
Even Such Is Time 1
William Shakespeare
Poor Soul, the Centre of My Sinful Earth 2
Fear No More the Heat o' the Sun 2
John Donne
Death, Be Not Proud 3
Ben Jonson
On My First Son 3
Robert Herrick
Eternity 4
Francis Quarles
A Good-Night 4
George Herbert
Virtue 4
John Milton
On Time 5
Richard Crashaw
An Epitaph Upon Husband and Wife 6
Henry Vaughan
They Are All Gone into the World of Light 6
Peace 7
Alexander Pope
The Dying Christian to His Soul 8
Ode on Solitude 8
William Cowper
Light Shining Out of Darkness 9
William Wordsworth
A Slumber Did My Spirit Seal 10
Walter Savage Landor
I Strove with None 10
Death 10

Felicia Dorothea Hemans
Dirge 10
John Clare
I Am 11
William Cullen Bryant
Thanatopsis 11
To the Fringed Gentian 13
Blessed Are They That Mourn 14
Hartley Coleridge
Early Death 15
Thomas Hood
The Death-Bed 15
John Henry, Cardinal Newman
Rest 16
Thomas Lovell Beddoes
Dirge 16
Edgar Allan Poe
To One in Paradise 17
Sarah Flower Adams
The Mourners Came at Break of Day 18
Elizabeth Barrett Browning
The Sleep 18
Charles Doyne Sillery
She Died in Beauty 19
Henry Wadsworth Longfellow
The Rainy Day 20
A Psalm of Life 20
Caroline Elizabeth Norton
Not Lost, But Gone Before 21
Edward FitzGerald
From The Rubaiyat of Omar Khayyám 22
Alfred Lord Tennyson
Crossing the Bar 23
From In Memoriam 24
James Aldrich
A Death-Bed 26
William Bell Scott
My Mother 27
Robert Browning
Prospice 27
Christopher Cranch
Enosis 28

Aubrey Thomas de Vere
Sorrow 29
Emily Brontë
No Coward Soul Is Mine 29
Sympathy 30
Remembrance 31
James Russell Lowell
The First Snow-Fall 32
Walt Whitman
At the Last, Tenderly 33
Darest Thou Now, O Soul 33
Matthew Arnold
Requiescat 34
Emily Dickinson
Because I Could Not Stop for Death 34
After Great Pain, a Formal Feeling Comes 35
I Never Saw a Moor 35
Christina Georgina Rossetti
Up-Hill 35
When I Am Dead 36
Remember 36
Rest 37
Elizabeth Akers
Endurance 37
James Thomson
A Requiem 38
Algernon Charles Swinburne
The Garden of Proserpine 39
Lizzie Clark Hardy
Some Time at Eve 41
John Addington Symonds
Lux Est Umbra Dei 42
Thomas Hardy
Transformations 42
The Darkling Thrush 43
Gerard Manley Hopkins
(Carrion Comfort) 44
John Banister Tabb
Evolution 44
William Ernest Henley
Invictus 45
James Whitcomb Riley
Away 45

Robert Louis Stevenson
Requiem 46
In Memoriam F. A. S. 46
John Davidson
Song 46
A. E. Housman
The Night Is Freezing Fast 47
To an Athlete Dying Young 47
With Rue My Heart Is Laden 48
George Santayana
To W. P. II 48
Rudyard Kipling
The Widower 49
Paul Laurence Dunbar
When All Is Done 49
Robert Frost
Acceptance 50
John Masefield
A Song at Parting 50
Edna St. Vincent Millay
Dirge Without Music 51
W. H. Auden
Funeral Blues 51
Dylan Thomas
Do Not Go Gentle into That Good Night 52

King James Bible

Psalm 23

The Lord is my shepherd; I shall not want.
He maketh me to lie down in green pastures: he leadeth me beside the still waters.
He restoreth my soul: he leadeth me in the paths of righteousness for his name's sake.
Yea, though I walk through the valley of the shadow of death, I will fear no evil: for thou art with me; thy rod and thy staff they comfort me.
Thou preparest a table before me in the presence of mine enemies: thou anointest my head with oil; my cup runneth over.
Surely goodness and mercy shall follow me all the days of my life: and I will dwell in the house of the Lord for ever.

Walter Raleigh (1554–1618)

Even Such Is Time

Even such is Time, that takes in trust
  Our youth, our joys, our all we have,
And pays us but with earth and dust;
  Who in the dark and silent grave,
When we have wandered all our ways,
Shuts up the story of our days;
But from this earth, this grave, this dust,
My God will raise me up, I trust.

William Shakespeare (1564–1616)

Poor Soul, the Centre of My Sinful Earth

Poor soul, the centre of my sinful earth,
Fooled by those rebel powers that thee array,
Why dost thou pine within and suffer dearth,
Painting thy outward walls so costly gay?
Why so large cost, having so short a lease,
Dost thou upon thy fading mansion spend?
Shall worms, inheritors of this excess,
Eat up thy charge? Is this thy body's end?
Then, soul, live thou upon thy servant's loss,
And let that pine to aggravate thy store;
Buy terms divine in selling hours of dross;
Within be fed, without be rich no more.
  So shalt thou feed on Death, that feeds on men,
  And, Death once dead, there's no more dying then.

Fear No More the Heat o' the Sun

Fear no more the heat o' the sun
  Nor the furious winter's rages;
Thou thy worldly task hast done,
  Home art gone and ta'en thy wages:
Golden lads and girls all must,
As chimney-sweepers, come to dust.

Fear no more the frown o' the great;
  Thou art past the tyrant's stroke;
Care no more to clothe and eat;
  To thee the reed is as the oak:
The sceptre, learning, physic, must
All follow this, and come to dust.

Fear no more the lightning-flash,
  Nor the all-dreaded thunder-stone;
Fear not slander, censure rash;
  Thou hast finished joy and moan:
All lovers young, all lovers must
Consign to thee, and come to dust.

No exorciser harm thee!
Nor no witchcraft charm thee!
Ghost unlaid forbear thee!
Nothing ill come near thee!
Quiet consummation have;
And renowned be thy grave!

John Donne (1572–1631)

Death, Be Not Proud

Death, be not proud, though some have called thee
Mighty and dreadful, for thou art not so:
For those whom thou think'st thou dost overthrow
Die not, poor Death; nor yet canst thou kill me.
From Rest and Sleep, which but thy picture be,
Much pleasure, then from thee much more must flow;
And soonest our best men with thee do go—
Rest of their bones and souls' delivery!
Thou'rt slave to fate, chance, kings, and desperate men,
And dost with poison, war, and sickness dwell;
And poppy or charms can make us sleep as well
And better than thy stroke. Why swell'st thou then?
One short sleep past, we wake eternally,
And Death shall be no more: Death, thou shalt die!

Ben Jonson (1572–1637)

On My First Son

Farewell, thou child of my right hand, and joy;
My sin was too much hope of thee, loved boy.
Seven years thou wert lent to me, and I thee pay,
Exacted by thy fate, on the just day.
Oh, could I lose all father now! For why
Will man lament the state he should envy?
To have so soon 'scaped world's and flesh's rage,
And if no other misery, yet age!
Rest in soft peace, and asked, say, Here doth lie
Ben Jonson his best piece of poetry.
For whose sake henceforth all his vows be such
As what he loves may never like too much.

Robert Herrick (1591–1674)

Eternity

O years! and Age! Farewell:
Behold I go,
Where I do know
Infinity to dwell.

And these mine eyes shall see
All times, how they
Are lost i' th' Sea
Of vast Eternity.

Where never Moon shall sway
The Stars; but she,
And Night, shall be
Drown'd in one endless Day.

Francis Quarles (1592–1644)

A Good-Night

Close now thine eyes and rest secure;
Thy soul is safe enough, thy body sure;
He that loves thee, he that keeps
And guards thee, never slumbers, never sleeps.
The smiling conscience in a sleeping breast
Has only peace, has only rest;
The music and the mirth of kings
Are all but very discords, when she sings;
Then close thine eyes and rest secure;
No sleep so sweet as thine, no rest so sure.

George Herbert (1593–1633)

Virtue

Sweet day, so cool, so calm, so bright!
The bridal of the earth and sky—
The dew shall weep thy fall to-night;
For thou must die.

Sweet rose, whose hue angry and brave
Bids the rash gazer wipe his eye,
Thy root is ever in its grave,
    And thou must die.

Sweet spring, full of sweet days and roses,
A box where sweets compacted lie,
My music shows ye have your closes,
    And all must die.

Only a sweet and virtuous soul,
Like season'd timber, never gives;
But though the whole world turn to coal,
    Then chiefly lives.

John Milton (1608–1674)

On Time

Fly envious Time, till thou run out thy race,
Call on the lazy leaden-stepping hours,
Whose speed is but the heavy Plummets pace;
And glut thy self with what thy womb devours,
Which is no more then what is false and vain,
And meerly mortal dross;
So little is our loss,
So little is thy gain.
For when as each thing bad thou hast entomb'd,
And last of all, thy greedy self consum'd,
Then long Eternity shall greet our bliss
With an individual kiss;
And Joy shall overtake us as a flood,
When every thing that is sincerely good,
And perfectly divine,
With Truth, and Peace, and Love shall ever shine
About the supreme Throne
Of him, t'whose happy-making sight alone,
When once our heav'nly-guided soul shall clime,
Then all this Earthy grosnes quit,
Attir'd with Stars, we shall for ever sit,
    Triumphing over Death, and Chance, and thee O Time.

Richard Crashaw (1613–1649)

An Epitaph Upon Husband and Wife Who died and were buried together.

To these whom death again did wed
This grave's the second marriage-bed.
For though the hand of Fate could force
'Twixt soul and body a divorce,
It could not sever man and wife,
Because they both lived but one life.
Peace, good reader, do not weep;
Peace, the lovers are asleep.
They, sweet turtles, folded lie
In the last knot that love could tie.
Let them sleep, let them sleep on,
Till the stormy night be gone,
And the eternal morrow dawn;
Then the curtains will be drawn,
And they wake into a light
Whose day shall never die in night.

Henry Vaughan (1621–1695)

They Are All Gone into the World of Light!

They are all gone into the world of light!
    And I alone sit ling'ring here;
Their very memory is fair and bright,
        And my sad thoughts doth clear.

It glows and glitters in my cloudy breast,
    Like stars upon some gloomy grove,
Or those faint beams in which this hill is drest
        After the sun's remove.

I see them walking in an air of glory,
    Whose light doth trample on my days:
My days, which are at best but dull and hoary,
        Mere glimmering and decays.

O holy Hope! and high Humility,
    High as the heavens above!
These are your walks, and you have show'd them me,
        To kindle my cold love.

Dear, beauteous Death! the jewel of the Just,
Shining nowhere, but in the dark;
What mysteries do lie beyond thy dust,
Could man outlook that mark!

He that hath found some fledg'd bird's nest may know,
At first sight, if the bird be flown;
But what fair well or grove he sings in now,
That is to him unknown.

And yet as Angels in some brighter dreams
Call to the soul, when man doth sleep;
So some strange thoughts transcend our wonted themes,
And into glory peep.

If a star were confin'd into a tomb,
Her captive flames must needs burn there;
But when the hand that lock'd her up gives room,
She'll shine through all the sphere.

O Father of eternal life, and all
Created glories under Thee!
Resume Thy spirit from this world of thrall
Into true liberty.

Either disperse these mists, which blot and fill
My perspective still as they pass:
Or else remove me hence unto that hill,
Where I shall need no glass.

Peace

My soul, there is a country
Far beyond the stars,
Where stands a wingèd sentry
All skilful in the wars:
There, above noise and danger,
Sweet Peace sits crown'd with smiles,
And One born in a mánger
Commands the beauteous files.
He is thy gracious Friend,
And—O my soul, awake!—
Did in pure love descend
To die here for thy sake.
If thou canst get but thither,
There grows the flower of Peace,

The Rose that cannot wither,
Thy fortress, and thy ease.
Leave then thy foolish ranges;
For none can thee secure
But One who never changes—
Thy God, thy life, thy cure.

Alexander Pope (1688–1744)

The Dying Christian to His Soul

Vital spark of heavenly flame,
Quit, O quit this mortal frame!
Trembling, hoping, lingering, flying,
O the pain, the bliss of dying!
Cease, fond Nature, cease thy strife,
And let me languish into life.

Hark! they whisper; angels say,
Sister Spirit, come away!
What is this absorbs me quite,
Steals my senses, shuts my sight,
Drowns my spirits, draws my breath?
Tell me, my soul, can this be death?

The world recedes; it disappears!
Heaven opens on my eyes; my ears
With sounds seraphic ring!
Lend, lend your wings! I mount! I fly!
O Grave! where is thy victory?
O Death! where is thy sting?

Ode on Solitude

Happy the man, whose wish and care
A few paternal acres bound,
Content to breathe his native air
In his own ground.

Whose herds with milk, whose fields with bread,
Whose flocks supply him with attire,
Whose trees in summer yield him shade,
In winter fire.

Blest, who can unconcern'dly find
   Hours, days, and years slide soft away,
In health of body, peace of mind,
               Quiet by day.

Sound sleep by night; study and ease,
   Together mixt; sweet recreation:
And innocence, which most does please
               With meditation.

Thus let me live, unseen, unknown,
   Thus unlamented let me die,
Steal from the world, and not a stone
               Tell where I lie.

William Cowper (1731–1800)

Light Shining Out of Darkness

God moves in a mysterious way,
   His wonders to perform;
He plants His footsteps in the sea,
   And rides upon the storm.

Deep in unfathomable mines
   Of never-failing skill
He treasures up His bright designs,
   And works His sovereign will.

Ye fearful saints, fresh courage take;
   The clouds ye so much dread
Are big with mercy, and shall break
   In blessings on your head.

Judge not the Lord by feeble sense,
   But trust Him for His grace;
Behind a frowning Providence
   He hides a smiling face.

His purposes will ripen fast,
   Unfolding every hour;
The bud may have a bitter taste,
   But sweet will be the flower.

Blind unbelief is sure to err,
  And scan His work in vain;
God is His own interpreter,
  And He will make it plain.

William Wordsworth (1770–1850)

A Slumber Did My Spirit Seal

A slumber did my spirit seal;
  I had no human fears;
She seemed a thing that could not feel
  The touch of earthly years.

No motion has she now, no force;
  She neither hears nor sees;
Rolled round in earth's diurnal course,
  With rocks, and stones, and trees.

Walter Savage Landor (1775–1864)

I Strove with None

I strove with none; for none was worth my strife.
Nature I loved and, next to Nature, Art;
I warmed both hands before the fire of life;
It sinks, and I am ready to depart.

Death

Death stands above me, whispering low
  I know not what into my ear;
Of his strange language all I know
  Is, there is not a word of fear.

Felicia Dorothea Hemans (1793–1835)

Dirge

Calm on the bosom of thy God,
  Fair spirit, rest thee now!
E'en while with ours thy footsteps trod,
  His seal was on thy brow.

Dust, to its narrow house beneath!
  Soul, to its place on high!
They that have seen thy look in death
  No more may fear to die.

Lone are the paths, and sad the bowers,
  Whence thy meek smile is gone;
But oh! a brighter home than ours
  In heaven, is now thine own.

John Clare (1793–1864)

I Am

I am: yet what I am none cares or knows,
  My friends forsake me like a memory lost;
I am the self-consumer of my woes,
  They rise and vanish in oblivious host,
Like shades in love and death's oblivion lost;
And yet I am, and live with shadows tost

Into the nothingness of scorn and noise,
  Into the living sea of waking dreams,
Where there is neither sense of life nor joys,
  But the vast shipwreck of my life's esteems;
And e'en the dearest—that I loved the best—
And strange—nay, rather stranger than the rest.

I long for scenes where man has never trod,
  A place where woman never smiled or wept;
There to abide with my Creator, God,
  And sleep as I in childhood sweetly slept:
Untroubled and untroubled where I lie,
The grass below—above the vaulted sky.

William Cullen Bryant (1794–1878)

Thanatopsis

To him who in the love of Nature holds
Communion with her visible forms, she speaks
A various language; for his gayer hours
She has a voice of gladness, and a smile
And eloquence of beauty, and she glides
Into his darker musings, with a mild

And healing sympathy, that steals away
Their sharpness, ere he is aware. When thoughts
Of the last bitter hour come like a blight
Over thy spirit, and sad images
Of the stern agony, and shroud, and pall,
And breathless darkness, and the narrow house,
Make thee to shudder and grow sick at heart;—
Go forth, under the open sky, and list
To Nature's teachings, while from all around—
Earth and her waters, and the depths of air—
Comes a still voice:—
                                        Yet a few days, and thee
The all-beholding sun shall see no more
In all his course; nor yet in the cold ground,
Where thy pale form was laid, with many tears,
Nor in the embrace of ocean, shall exist
Thy image. Earth, that nourished thee, shall claim
Thy growth, to be resolved to earth again,
And, lost each human trace, surrendering up
Thine individual being, shalt thou go
To mix forever with the elements,
To be a brother to the insensible rock
And to the sluggish clod, which the rude swain
Turns with his share, and treads upon. The oak
Shall send his roots abroad, and pierce thy mold.

   Yet not to thine eternal resting-place
Shalt thou retire alone, nor couldst thou wish
Couch more magnificent. Thou shalt lie down
With patriarchs of the infant world—with kings,
The powerful of the earth—the wise, the good,
Fair forms, and hoary seers of ages past,
All in one mighty sepulcher. The hills
Rock-ribbed and ancient as the sun,—the vales
Stretching in pensive quietness between;
The venerable woods—rivers that move
In majesty, and the complaining brooks
That make the meadows green; and, poured round all
Old Ocean's gray and melancholy waste,—
Are but the solemn decorations all
Of the great tomb of man. The golden sun,
The planets, all the infinite host of heaven,
Are shining on the sad abodes of death

Through the still lapse of ages. All that tread
The globe are but a handful to the tribes
That slumber in its bosom.—Take the wings
Of morning, pierce the Barcan wilderness,
Or lose thyself in the continuous woods
Where rolls the Oregon, and hears no sound,
Save his own dashings—yet the dead are there:
And millions in those solitudes, since first
The flight of years began, have laid them down
In their last sleep—the dead reign there alone.
So shalt thou rest, and what if thou withdraw
In silence from the living, and no friend
Take note of thy departure? All that breathe
Will share thy destiny. The gay will laugh
When thou art gone, the solemn brood of care
Plod on, and each one as before will chase
His favorite phantom; yet all these shall leave
Their mirth and their employments, and shall come
And make their bed with thee. As the long train
Of ages glides away, the sons of men—
The youth in life's fresh spring, and he who goes
In the full strength of years, matron and maid,
The speechless babe, and the gray-headed man—
Shall one by one be gathered to thy side,
By those, who in their turn shall follow them.

So live, that when thy summons comes to join
The innumerable caravan, which moves
To that mysterious realm, where each shall take
His chamber in the silent halls of death,
Thou go not, like the quarry-slave at night,
Scourged to his dungeon, but, sustained and soothed
By an unfaltering trust, approach thy grave
Like one who wraps the drapery of his couch
About him, and lies down to pleasant dreams.

To the Fringed Gentian

Thou blossom bright with autumn dew,
And colored with the heaven's own blue,
That openest when the quiet light
Succeeds the keen and frosty night.

Thou comest not when violets lean
O'er wandering brooks and springs unseen,
Or columbines, in purple dressed,
Nod o'er the ground-bird's hidden nest.

Thou waitest late and com'st alone,
When woods are bare and birds are flown,
And frost and shortening days portend
The aged year is near his end.

Then doth thy sweet and quiet eye
Look through its fringes to the sky,
Blue—blue—as if that sky let fall
A flower from its cerulean wall.

I would that thus, when I shall see
The hour of death draw near to me,
Hope, blossoming within my heart,
May look to heaven as I depart.

Blessed Are They That Mourn

Oh, deem not they are blest alone
  Whose lives a peaceful tenor keep;
The Power who pities man, has shown
  A blessing for the eyes that weep.

The light of smiles shall fill again
  The lids that overflow with tears;
And weary hours of woe and pain
  Are promises of happier years.

There is a day of sunny rest
  For every dark and troubled night;
And grief may bide an evening guest,
  But joy shall come with early light.

And thou, who o'er thy friend's low bier
  Dost shed the bitter drops like rain,
Hope that a brighter, happier sphere
  Will give him to thy arms again.

Nor let the good man's trust depart,
  Though life its common gifts deny,—
Though with a pierced and bleeding heart,
  And spurned of men, he goes to die.

For God hath marked each sorrowing day
And numbered every secret tear,
And heaven's long age of bliss shall pay
For all his children suffer here.

Hartley Coleridge (1796–1849)

Early Death

She passed away like morning dew
Before the sun was high;
So brief her time, she scarcely knew
The meaning of a sigh.

As round the rose its soft perfume,
Sweet love around her floated;
Admired she grew—while mortal doom
Crept on, unfeared, unnoted.

Love was her guardian Angel here,
But Love to Death resigned her;
Though Love was kind, why should we fear
But holy Death is kinder?

Thomas Hood (1799–1845)

The Death-Bed

We watched her breathing through the night,
Her breathing soft and low,
As in her breast the wave of life
Kept heaving to and fro.

So silently we seemed to speak,
So slowly moved about,
As we had lent her half our powers
To eke her living out.

Our very hopes belied our fears,
Our fears our hopes belied—
We thought her dying when she slept,
And sleeping when she died.

For when the morn came dim and sad,
And chill with early showers,
Her quiet eyelids closed—she had
Another morn than ours.

John Henry, Cardinal Newman (1801–1890)

Rest

They are at rest.
We may not stir the heaven of their repose
By rude invoking voice, or prayer addrest
In waywardness to those
Who in the mountain grots of Eden lie,
And hear the fourfold river as it murmurs by.

They hear it sweep
In distance down the dark and savage vale;
But they at rocky bed or current deep
Shall never more grow pale.
They hear, and meekly muse, as fain to know
How long untired, unspent, that giant stream shall flow.

And soothing sounds
Blend with the neighb'ring waters as they glide;
Posted along the haunted garden's bounds,
Angelic forms abide,
Echoing, as words of watch, o'er lawn and grove
The verses of that hymn which seraphs chant above.

Thomas Lovell Beddoes (1803–1849)

Dirge

Sorrow, lie still and wear
No tears, no sighings, no despair,
No mourning weeds,
Nought that discloses
A heart that bleeds;

But looks contented I will bear,
  And o'er my cheeks strew roses.
Unto the world I may not weep,
But save my sorrow all, and keep
  A secret heart, sweet soul, for thee,
  As the great earth and swelling sea—

Edgar Allan Poe (1804–1849)

To One in Paradise

Thou wast all that to me, love,
  For which my soul did pine—
A green isle in the sea, love,
  A fountain and a shrine,
All wreathed with fairy fruits and flowers,
  And all the flowers were mine.

Ah, dream too bright to last!
  Ah, starry Hope! that didst arise
But to be overcast!
  A voice from out the Future cries,
'On! on!'—but o'er the Past
  (Dim gulf!) my spirit hovering lies
Mute, motionless, aghast!

For, alas! alas! with me
  The light of Life is o'er!
  'No more—no more—no more—
(Such language holds the solemn sea
  To the sands upon the shore)
Shall bloom the thunder-blasted tree
  Or the stricken eagle soar!

And all my days are trances,
  And all my nightly dreams
Are where thy grey eye glances,
  And where thy footstep gleams—
In what ethereal dances,
  By what eternal streams.

Sarah Flower Adams (1805–1848)

The Mourners Came at Break of Day

The mourners came at break of day
Unto the garden-sepulcher;
With darkened hearts to weep and pray,
For Him, the loved one buried there.
What radiant light dispels the gloom?
An angel sits beside the tomb.

The earth doth mourn her treasures lost,
All sepulchered beneath the snow;
When wintry winds, and chilling frost
Have laid her summer glories low;
The spring returns, the flowerets bloom—
An angel sits beside the tomb.

Then mourn we not belovèd dead,
E'en while we come to weep and pray;
The happy spirit far hath fled
To brighter realms of endless day:
Immortal Hope dispels the gloom!
An angel sits beside the tomb.

Elizabeth Barrett Browning (1806–1867)

The Sleep

"He giveth his belovèd sleep."—PSALM cxxvii. 2.

Of all the thoughts of God that are
Borne inward unto souls afar,
Among the Psalmist's music deep,
Now tell me if that any is,
For gift or grace, surpassing this,—
"He giveth his belovèd sleep"?

What would we give to our beloved?
The hero's heart, to be unmoved,—
The poet's star-tuned harp, to sweep,—
The patriot's voice, to teach and rouse,—
The monarch's crown, to light the brows?
"He giveth *his* belovèd sleep."

What do we give to our beloved?
A little faith, all undisproved,—
A little dust to overweep,
And bitter memories, to make
The whole earth blasted for our sake,
"He giveth *his* belovèd sleep."

"Sleep soft, beloved!" we sometimes say,
But have no tune to charm away
Sad dreams that through the eyelids creep;
But never doleful dream again
Shall break the happy slumber when
"He giveth *his* belovèd sleep."

O earth, so full of dreary noise!
O men, with wailing in your voice!
O delvèd gold the wailers heap!
O strife, O curse, that o'er it fall!
God strikes a silence through you all,
"He giveth his belovèd sleep."

His dews drop mutely on the hill,
His cloud above it saileth still,
Though on its slope men sow and reap;
More softly than the dew is shed,
Or cloud is floated overhead,
"He giveth his belovèd sleep."

For me, my heart, that erst did go
Most like a tired child at a show,
That sees through tears the mummers leap,
Would now its wearied vision close,
Would childlike on his love repose
Who "giveth his belovèd sleep."

Charles Doyne Sillery (1807–1837)

She Died in Beauty

She died in beauty,—like a rose
  Blown from its parent stem;
She died in beauty,—like a pearl
  Dropped from some diadem.

She died in beauty,—like a lay
  Along a moonlit lake;
She died in beauty,—like the song
  On birds amid the brake.

She died in beauty,—like the snow
  On flowers dissolved away;
She died in beauty,—like a star
  Lost on the brow of day.

She lives in glory,—like night's gems
  Set round the silver moon;
She lives in glory,—like the sun
  Amid the blue of June.

Henry Wadsworth Longfellow (1807–1882)

The Rainy Day

The day is cold, and dark, and dreary;
It rains, and the wind is never weary;
The vine still clings to the moldering wall,
But at every gust the dead leaves fall,
  And the day is dark and dreary.

My life is cold, and dark, and dreary;
It rains, and the wind is never weary;
My thoughts still cling to the moldering Past,
But the hopes of youth fall thick in the blast
  And the days are dark and dreary.

Be still, sad heart! and cease repining;
Behind the clouds is the sun still shining;
  Thy fate is the common fate of all,
Into each life some rain must fall,
  Some days must be dark and dreary.

A Psalm of Life

What the heart of the young man said to the psalmist

Tell me not, in mournful numbers,
  Life is but an empty dream!—
For the soul is dead that slumbers,
  And things are not what they seem.

Life is real! Life is earnest!
And the grave is not its goal;
Dust thou art, to dust returnest,
Was not spoken of the soul.

Not enjoyment, and not sorrow,
Is our destined end or way;
But to act, that each to-morrow
Find us farther than to-day.

Art is long, and Time is fleeting,
And our hearts, though stout and brave,
Still, like muffled drums, are beating
Funeral marches to the grave.

In the world's broad field of battle,
In the bivouac of Life,
Be not like dumb, driven cattle!
Be a hero in the strife!

Trust no Future, howe'er pleasant!
Let the dead Past bury its dead!
Act,—act in the living Present!
Heart within, and God o'erhead!

Lives of great men all remind us
We can make our lives sublime,
And, departing, leave behind us
Footprints on the sands of time;

Footprints, that perhaps another,
Sailing o'er life's solemn main,
A forlorn and shipwrecked brother,
Seeing, shall take heart again.

Let us, then, be up and doing,
With a heart for any fate;
Still achieving, still pursuing,
Learn to labor and to wait.

Caroline Elizabeth Norton (1808–1877)

Not Lost, But Gone Before

How mournful seems, in broken dreams,
The memory of the day,
When icy Death hath sealed the breath
Of some dear form of clay.

When pale, unmoved, the face we loved,
  The face we thought so fair,
And the hand lies cold, whose fervent hold
  Once charmed away despair.

Oh, what could heal the grief we feel
  For hopes that come no more,
Had we ne'er heard the Scripture word,
  "Not lost, but gone before."

Oh, sadly yet with vain regret
  The widowed heart must yearn;
And mothers weep their babes asleep
  In the sunlight's vain return.

The brother's heart shall rue to part
  From the one through childhood known;
And the orphan's tears lament for years
  A friend and father gone.

For death and life, with ceaseless strife,
  Beat wild on this world's shore,
And all our calm is in that balm,
  "Not lost, but gone before."

Oh! world wherein nor death, nor sin,
  Nor weary warfare dwells;
Their blessed home we parted from
  With sobs and sad farewells.

Where eyes awake, for whose dear sake
  Our own with tears grow dim,
And faint accords of dying words
  Are changed for heaven's sweet hymn;

Oh! there at last, life's trials past,
  We'll meet our loved once more,
Whose feet have trod the path to God—
  "Not lost, but gone before."

Edward FitzGerald (1809–1883)

From **The Rubaiyat of Omar Khayyám**

Ah, my Beloved, fill the Cup that clears
TO-DAY of past Regrets and Future Fears:
  To-morrow!—Why, To-morrow I may be
Myself with Yesterday's Sev'n thousand Years.

For some we loved, the loveliest and the best
That from his Vintage rolling Time hath prest,
 Have drunk their Cup a Round or two before,
And one by one crept silently to rest.

And we, that now make merry in the Room
They left, and Summer dresses in new bloom,
 Ourselves must we beneath the Couch of Earth
Descend—ourselves to make a Couch—for whom?

Ah, make the most of what we yet may spend,
Before we too into the Dust descend;
 Dust unto dust, and under Dust to lie,
Sans Wine, sans Song, sans Singer, and—sans End!

• • •

Ah, with the Grape my fading Life provide,
And wash my Body whence the Life has died,
 And lay me, shrouded in the living Leaf,
By some not unfrequented Garden-side! . . .

Yon rising Moon that looks for us again—
How oft hereafter will she wax and wane;
 How oft hereafter rising look for us
Through this same Garden—and for *one* in vain!

And when like her, O Sáki, you shall pass
Among the Guests star-scatter'd on the Grass,
 And in your joyous errand reach the spot
Where I made One—turn down an empty Glass!

Alfred Lord Tennyson (1809–1892)

Crossing the Bar

Sunset and evening star,
 And one clear call for me!
And may there be no moaning of the bar,
 When I put out to sea,

But such a tide as moving seems asleep,
 Too full for sound and foam,
When that which drew from out the boundless deep
 Turns again home.

Twilight and evening bell,
 And after that the dark!

And may there be no sadness of farewell,
   When I embark;

For though from out our bourne of Time and Place
   The flood may bear me far,
I hope to see my Pilot face to face
   When I have crossed the bar.

From **In Memoriam**

57

Peace; come away: the song of woe
   Is after all an earthly song.
   Peace; come away: we do him wrong
To sing so wildly; let us go.

Come, let us go; your cheeks are pale;
   But half my life I leave behind.
   Methinks my friend is richly shrined;
But I shall pass, my work will fail.

Yet in these ears, till hearing dies,
   One set slow bell will seem to toll
   The passing of the sweetest soul
That ever looked with human eyes.

I hear it now, and o'er and o'er,
   Eternal greetings to the dead;
   And "Ave, Ave, Ave," said,
"Adieu, adieu," forevermore.

58

In those sad words I took farewell.
   Like echoes in sepulchral halls,
   As drop by drop the water falls
In vaults and catacombs, they fell;

And, falling, idly broke the peace
   Of hearts that beat from day to day,
   Half-conscious of their dying clay,
And those cold crypts where they shall cease.

The high Muse answered: "Wherefore grieve
   Thy brethren with a fruitless tear?
   Abide a little longer here,
And thou shalt take a nobler leave."

59

O Sorrow, wilt thou live with me
  No casual mistress, but a wife,
  My bosom-friend and half of life;
As I confess it needs must be;

O Sorrow, wilt thou rule my blood,
  Be sometimes lovely like a bride,
  And put thy harsher moods aside,
If thou wilt have me wise and good.

My centered passion cannot move,
  Nor will it lessen from today;
  But I'll have leave at times to play
As with the creature of my love;

And set thee forth, for thou art mine,
  With so much hope for years to come,
  That, howsoe'er I know thee, some
Could hardly tell what name were thine.

• • •

129

Dear friend, far off, my lost desire,
  So far, so near in woe and weal,
  O loved the most, when most I feel
There is a lower and a higher;

Known and unknown, human, divine;
  Sweet human hand and lips and eye;
  Dear heavenly friend that canst not die,
Mine, mine, forever, ever mine;

Strange friend, past, present, and to be;
  Loved deeplier, darklier understood;
  Behold, I dream a dream of good,
And mingle all the world with thee.

130

Thy voice is on the rolling air;
  I hear thee where the waters run;
  Thou standest in the rising sun,
And in the setting thou art fair.

What art thou then? I cannot guess;
  But though I seem in star and flower
  To feel thee some diffusive power,
I do not therefore love thee less.

My love involves the love before;
My love is vaster passion now;
Though mixed with God and Nature thou,
I seem to love thee more and more.

Far off thou art, but ever nigh;
I have thee still, and I rejoice;
I prosper, circled with thy voice;
I shall not lose thee though I die.

131

O living will that shalt endure
When all that seems shall suffer shock,
Rise in the spiritual rock,
Flow through our deeds and make them pure,

That we may lift from out of dust
A voice as unto him that hears,
A cry above the conquered years
To one that with us works, and trust,

With faith that comes of self-control,
The truths that never can be proved
Until we close with all we loved,
And all we flow from, soul in soul.

James Aldrich (1810–1856)

A Death-Bed

Her suffering ended with the day,
Yet lived she at its close,
And breathed the long, long night away
In statue-like repose.

But when the sun in all his state
Illumed the eastern skies,
She passed through Glory's morning gate
And walked in Paradise.

William Bell Scott (1811–1890)

My Mother

There was a gather'd stillness in the room:
Only the breathing of the great sea rose
From far off, aiding that profound repose,
With regular pulse and pause within the gloom
Of twilight, as if some impending doom
Was now approaching;—I sat moveless there,
Watching with tears and thoughts that were like prayer,
Till the hour struck,—the thread dropp'd from the loom;
And the Bark pass'd in which freed souls are borne.
The dear still'd face lay there; that sound forlorn
Continued; I rose not, but long sat by:
And now my heart oft hears that sad seashore,
When she is in the far-off land, and I
Wait the dark sail returning yet once more.

Robert Browning (1812–1889)

Prospice

Fear death?—to feel the fog in my throat,
  The mist in my face,
When the snows begin, and the blasts denote
  I am nearing the place,
The power of the night, the press of the storm,
  The post of the foe;
Where he stands, the Arch Fear in a visible form,
  Yet the strong man must go:
For the journey is done and the summit attained,
  And the barriers fall,
Though a battle's to fight ere the guerdon be gained,
  The reward of it all.
I was ever a fighter, so—one fight more,
  The best and the last!
I would hate that death bandaged my eyes, and forbore,
  And bade me creep past.

No! let me taste the whole of it, fare like my peers
The heroes of old,
Bear the brunt, in a minute pay glad life's arrears
Of pain, darkness and cold.
For sudden the worst turns the best to the brave,
The black minute's at end,
And the elements' rage, the fiend-voices that rave,
Shall dwindle, shall blend,
Shall change, shall become first a peace out of pain,
Then a light, then thy breast,
O thou soul of my soul! I shall clasp thee again,
And with God be the rest!

Christopher Cranch (1813–1892)

Enosis

Thought is deeper than all speech,
Feeling deeper than all thought;
Souls to souls can never teach
What unto themselves was taught.

We are spirits clad in veils;
Man by man was never seen;
All our deep communing fails
To remove the shadowy screen.

Heart to heart was never known;
Mind with mind did never meet;
We are columns left alone,
Of a temple once complete.

Like the stars that gem the sky,
Far apart, though seeming near,
In our light we scattered lie;
All is thus but starlight here.

What is social company
But a babbling summer stream?
What our wise philosophy
But the glancing of a dream?

Only when the sun of love
Melts the scattered stars of thought;

Only when we live above
  What the dim-eyed world hath taught;

Only when our souls are fed
  By the Fount which gave them birth,
And by inspiration led,
  Which they never drew from earth,

We like parted drops of rain
  Swelling till they meet and run,
Shall be all absorbed again,
  Melting, flowing into one.

Aubrey Thomas de Vere (1814–1902)

Sorrow

Count each affliction, whether light or grave,
  God's messenger sent down to thee; do thou
  With courtesy receive him; rise and bow;
And, ere his shadow pass thy threshold, crave
Permission first his heavenly feet to lave;
  Then lay before him all thou hast; allow
  No cloud of passion to usurp thy brow,
Or mar thy hospitality; no wave
Of mortal tumult to obliterate
  The soul's marmoreal calmness: Grief should be,
Like joy, majestic, equable, sedate;
  Confirming, cleansing, raising, making free;
Strong to consume small troubles; to commend
Great thoughts, grave thoughts, thoughts lasting to the end.

Emily Brontë (1818–1848)

No Coward Soul Is Mine

  No coward soul is mine,
No trembler in the world's storm-troubled sphere:
  I see Heaven's glories shine,
And faith shines equal, arming me from fear.

O God within my breast,
Almighty, ever-present Deity!
Life—that in me has rest,
As I—undying Life—have power in Thee!

Vain are the thousand creeds
That move men's hearts: unutterably vain;
Worthless as withered weeds,
Or idlest froth amid the boundless main,

To waken doubt in one
Holding so fast by Thine infinity;
So surely anchored on
The steadfast rock of immortality.

With wide-embracing love
Thy Spirit animates eternal years,
Pervades and broods above,
Changes, sustains, dissolves, creates, and rears.

Though earth and man were gone,
And suns and universes cease to be,
And Thou were left alone,
Every existence would exist in Thee.

There is not room for Death,
Nor atom that his might could render void:
Thou—Thou art Being and Breath,
And what Thou art may never be destroyed.

Sympathy

There should be no despair for you
While nightly stars are burning;
While evening pours its silent dew
nd sunshine gilds the morning.
There should be no despair—though tears
May flow down like a river:
Are not the best beloved of years
Around your heart for ever?

They weep, you weep, it must be so;
Winds sigh as you are sighing,
And Winter sheds his grief in snow
Where Autumn's leaves are lying:

Yet, these revive, and from their fate
Your fate cannot be parted:
Then, journey on, if not elate,
Still, *never* broken-hearted!

Remembrance

Cold in the earth—and the deep snow piled above thee,
Far, far, removed, cold in the dreary grave!
Have I forgot, my only Love, to love thee,
Severed at last by Time's all-severing wave?

Now, when alone, do my thoughts no longer hover
Over the mountains, on that northern shore,
Resting their wings where heath and fern-leaves cover
Thy noble heart for ever, ever more?

Cold in the earth—and fifteen wild Decembers,
From those brown hills, have melted into spring:
Faithful, indeed, is the spirit that remembers
After such years of change and suffering!

Sweet Love of youth, forgive, if I forget thee,
While the world's tide is bearing me along;
Other desires and other hopes beset me,
Hopes which obscure, but cannot do thee wrong!

No later light has lightened up my heaven,
No second morn has ever shone for me;
All my life's bliss from thy dear life was given,
All my life's bliss is in the grave with thee.

But, when the days of golden dreams had perished,
And even Despair was powerless to destroy;
Then did I learn how existence could be cherished,
Strengthened, and fed without the aid of joy.

Then did I check the tears of useless passion—
Weaned my young soul from yearning after thine;
Sternly denied its burning wish to hasten
Down to that tomb already more than mine.

And, even yet, I dare not let it languish,
Dare not indulge in memory's rapturous pain;
Once drinking deep of that divinest anguish,
How could I seek the empty world again?

James Russell Lowell (1819–1891)

The First Snow-Fall

The snow had begun in the gloaming,
And busily all the night
Had been heaping field and highway
With a silence deep and white.

Every pine and fir and hemlock
Wore ermine too dear for an earl,
And the poorest twig on the elm-tree
Was ridged inch deep with pearl.

From sheds new-roofed with Carrara
Came Chanticleer's muffled crow,
The stiff rails were softened to swan's-down,
And still fluttered down the snow.

I stood and watched by the window
The noiseless work of the sky,
And the sudden flurries of snow-birds,
Like brown leaves whirling by.

I thought of a mound in sweet Auburn
Where a little headstone stood;
How the flakes were folding it gently,
As did robins the babes in the wood.

Up spoke our own little Mabel,
Saying, "Father, who makes it snow?"
And I told of the good All-father
Who cares for us here below.

Again I looked at the snow-fall,
And thought of the leaden sky
That arched o'er our first great sorrow,
When that mound was heaped so high.

I remember the gradual patience
That fell from that cloud like snow,
Flake by flake, healing and hiding
The scar of our deep-plunged woe.

And again to the child I whispered,
"The snow that husheth all,
Darling, the merciful Father
Alone can make it fall!"

Then, with eyes that saw not, I kissed her;
And she, kissing back, could not know
That *my* kiss was given to her sister,
Folded close under deepening snow.

Walt Whitman (1819–1892)

At the Last, Tenderly

At the last, tenderly,
From the walls of the powerful, fortressed house,
From the clasp of the knitted locks, from the keep of the well-closed doors,
Let me be wafted.

Let me glide noiselessly forth;
With the key of softness unlock the locks—with a whisper
Set ope the doors, O soul!

Tenderly—be not impatient!
(Strong is your hold, O mortal flesh!
Strong is your hold, O love!)

Darest Thou Now, O Soul

Darest thou now, O soul,
Walk out with me toward the unknown region,
Where neither ground is for the feet nor any path to follow?

No map there, nor guide,
Nor voice sounding, nor touch of human hand,
Nor face with blooming flesh, nor lips, nor eyes, are in that land.

I know it not, O soul,
Nor dost thou, all is a blank before us,—
All waits undreamed of in that region, that inaccessible land.

Till when the ties loosen,
All but the ties eternal, Time and Space,
Nor darkness, gravitation, sense, nor any bounds bounding us.

Then we burst forth, we float,
In Time and Space, O soul! prepared for them,
Equal, equipped at last (O joy! O fruit of all!), them to fulfill, O soul!

Matthew Arnold (1822–1888)

Requiescat

Strew on her roses, roses,
    And never a spray of yew.
In quiet she reposes:
    Ah! would that I did too.

Her mirth the world required:
    She bathed it in smiles of glee.
But her heart was tired, tired,
    And now they let her be.

Her life was turning, turning,
    In mazes of heat and sound.
But for peace her soul was yearning,
    And now peace laps her round.

Her cabined, ample Spirit,
    It fluttered and failed for breath.
To-night it doth inherit
    The vasty Hall of Death.

Emily Dickinson (1830–1886)

Because I Could Not Stop for Death

Because I could not stop for Death,
He kindly stopped for me;
The carriage held but just ourselves
And Immortality.

We slowly drove, he knew no haste,
And I had put away
My labor, and my leisure too,
For his civility.

We passed the school where children played,
Their lessons scarcely done;
We passed the fields of gazing grain,
We passed the setting sun.

We paused before a house that seemed
A swelling of the ground;
The roof was scarcely visible,
The cornice but a mound.

Since then 't is centuries; but each
Feels shorter than the day
I first surmised the horses' heads
Were toward eternity.

After Great Pain, a Formal Feeling Comes

After great pain, a formal feeling comes:
The Nerves sit ceremonious, like Tombs;
The stiff Heart questions was it He, that bore,
And Yesterday, or Centuries before?

The Feet, mechanical, go round—
Of Ground, or Air, or Ought—
A Wooden way
Regardless grown,
A Quartz contentment, like a stone.

This is the Hour of Lead,
Remembered, if outlived,
As Freezing persons, recollect the Snows:
First—Chill—then Stupor—then the letting go.

I Never Saw a Moor

I never saw a moor,
I never saw the sea;
Yet know I how the heather looks,
And what a wave must be.

I never spoke with God,
Nor visited in heaven;
Yet certain am I of the spot
As if the chart were given.

Christina Georgina Rossetti (1830–1894)

Up-Hill

Does the road wind up-hill all the way?
  Yes, to the very end.
Will the day's journey take the whole long day?
  From morn to night, my friend.

But is there for the night a resting-place?
  A roof for when the slow, dark hours begin.
May not the darkness hide it from my face?
  You cannot miss that inn.

Shall I meet other wayfarers at night?
  Those who have gone before.
Then must I knock, or call when just in sight?
  They will not keep you waiting at that door.

Shall I find comfort, travel-sore and weak?
  Of labor you shall find the sum.
Will there be beds for me and all who seek?
  Yea, beds for all who come.

When I Am Dead

When I am dead, my dearest,
  Sing no sad songs for me;
Plant thou no roses at my head,
  Nor shady cypress tree:
Be the green grass above me
  With showers and dewdrops wet;
And if thou wilt, remember,
  And if thou wilt, forget.

I shall not see the shadows,
  I shall not feel the rain;
I shall not hear the nightingale
  Sing on, as if in pain:
And dreaming through the twilight
  That doth not rise nor set,
Haply I may remember,
  And haply may forget.

Remember

Remember me when I am gone away,
  Gone far away into the silent land;
  When you can no more hold me by the hand,
Nor I half turn to go yet turning stay.
Remember me when no more day by day
  You tell me of our future that you planned:
  Only remember me; you understand
It will be late to counsel then or pray.
Yet if you should forget me for a while

And afterwards remember, do not grieve:
For if the darkness and corruption leave
A vestige of the thoughts that once I had,
Better by far you should forget and smile
Than that you should remember and be sad.

Rest

O Earth, lie heavily upon her eyes;
Seal her sweet eyes weary of watching, Earth;
Lie close around her; leave no room for mirth
With its harsh laughter, nor for sound of sighs.
She hath no questions, she hath no replies,
Hush'd in and curtain'd with a blessèd dearth
Of all that irk'd her from the hour of birth;
With stillness that is almost Paradise.
Darkness more clear than noonday holdeth her,
Silence more musical than any song;
Even her very heart has ceased to stir:
Until the morning of Eternity
Her rest shall not begin nor end, but be;
And when she wakes she will not think it long.

Elizabeth Akers (1832–1911)

Endurance

How much the heart may bear, and yet not break!
How much the flesh may suffer, and not die!
I question much if any pain or ache
Of soul or body brings our end more nigh:
Death chooses his own time; till that is sworn,
All evils may be borne.

We shrink and shudder at the surgeon's knife,
Each nerve recoiling from the cruel steel
Whose edge seems searching for the quivering life;
Yet to our sense the bitter pangs reveal,
That still, although the trembling flesh be torn,
This also can be borne.

We see a sorrow rising in our way,
And try to flee from the approaching ill;
We seek some small escape: we weep and pray;
But when the blow falls, then our hearts are still;

Not that the pain is of its sharpness shorn,
But that it can be borne.

We wind our life about another life;
We hold it closer, dearer than our own:
Anon it faints and fails in deathly strife,
Leaving us stunned and stricken and alone;
But ah! we do not die with those we mourn,—
This also can be borne.

Behold, we live through all things,—famine, thirst,
Bereavement, pain; all grief and misery,
All woe and sorrow; life inflicts its worst
On soul and body,—but we can not die.
Though we be sick, and tired, and faint, and worn,—
Lo, all things can be borne!

James Thomson (1834–1882)

A Requiem

Thou hast lived in pain and woe,
Thou hast lived in grief and fear;
Now thine heart can dread no blow,
Now thine eyes can shed no tear;
Storms round us shall beat and rave;
Thou art sheltered in the grave.

Thou for long, long years hast borne,
Bleeding through Life's wilderness,
Heavy loss and wounding scorn;
Now thine heart is burdenless:
Vainly rest for ours we crave;
Thine is quiet in the grave.

We must toil with pain and care,
We must front tremendous Fate,
We must fight with dark Despair:
Thou dost dwell in solemn state,
Couched triumphant, calm and brave,
In the ever-holy grave.

Algernon Charles Swinburne (1837–1909)

The Garden of Proserpine

Here, where the world is quiet;
  Here, where all trouble seems
Dead winds' and spent waves' riot
  In doubtful dreams of dreams;
I watch the green field growing
For reaping folk and sowing,
For harvest-time and mowing,
  A sleepy world of streams.

I am tired of tears and laughter,
  And men that laugh and weep,
Of what may come hereafter
  For men that sow to reap;
I am weary of days and hours,
Blown buds of barren flowers,
Desires and dreams and powers
  And everything but sleep.

Here life has death for neighbor,
  And far from eye or ear
Wan waves and wet winds labor,
  Weak ships and spirits steer;
They drive adrift, and whither
They wot not who make thither;
But no such winds blow hither,
  And no such things grow here.

No growth of moor or coppice,
  No heather-flower or vine,
But bloomless buds of poppies,
  Green grapes of Proserpine,
Pale beds of blowing rushes
Where no leaf blooms or blushes
Save this whereout she crushes
  For dead men deadly wine.

Pale, without name or number,
  In fruitless fields of corn,
They bow themselves and slumber
  All night till light is born;

And like a soul belated,
In hell and heaven unmated,
By cloud and mist abated
  Comes out of darkness morn.

Though one were strong as seven,
  He too with death shall dwell,
Nor wake with wings in heaven,
  Nor weep for pains in hell;
Though one were fair as roses,
His beauty clouds and closes;
And well though love reposes,
  In the end it is not well.

Pale, beyond porch and portal,
  Crowned with calm leaves, she stands
Who gathers all things mortal
  With cold immortal hands;
Her languid lips are sweeter
Than love's who fears to greet her
To men that mix and meet her
  From many times and lands.

She waits for each and other,
  She waits for all men born;
Forgets the earth her mother,
  The life of fruits and corn;
And spring and seed and swallow
Take wing for her and follow
Where summer song rings hollow
  And flowers are put to scorn.

There go the loves that wither,
  The old loves with wearier wings;
And all dead years draw thither,
  And all disastrous things;
Dead dreams of days forsaken,
Blind buds that snows have shaken,
Wild leaves that winds have taken,
  Red strays of ruined springs.

We are not sure of sorrow,
  And joy was never sure;
Today will die tomorrow;
  Time stoops to no man's lure;

And love, grown faint and fretful,
With lips but half regretful
Sighs, and with eyes forgetful
  Weeps that no loves endure.

From too much love of living,
  From hope and fear set free,
We thank with brief thanksgiving
  Whatever gods may be
That no life lives forever;
That dead men rise up never;
That even the weariest river
  Winds somewhere safe to sea.

Then star nor sun shall waken,
  Nor any change of light;
Nor sound of waters shaken,
  Nor any sound or sight;
Nor wintry leaves nor vernal,
Not days nor things diurnal;
  Only the sleep eternal
  In an eternal night.

Lizzie Clark Hardy (dates unknown)

Some Time at Eve

Some time at eve when the tide is low,
  I shall slip my mooring and sail away,
With no response to the friendly hail
  Of kindred craft in the busy bay.
In the silent hush of the twilight pale,
  When the night stoops down to embrace the day,
And the voices call in the waters' flow—
Some time at eve when the tide is low,
  I shall slip my mooring and sail away.

Through the purpling shadows that darkly trail
  O'er the ebbing tide of the Unknown Sea,
I shall fare me away, with a dip of sail
And a ripple of waters to tell the tale
  Of a lonely voyager, sailing away
  To the Mystic Isles where at anchor lay
The crafts of those who have sailed before
O'er the Unknown Sea to the Unseen Shore.

A few who have watched me sail away
Will miss my craft from the busy bay;
  Some friendly barks that were anchored near,
  Some loving souls that my heart held dear,
  In silent sorrow will drop a tear—

But I shall have peacefully furled my sail
In moorings sheltered from storm or gale,
  And greeted the friends who have sailed before
  O'er the Unknown Sea to the Unseen Shore.

John Addington Symonds (1840–1893)

Lux Est Umbra Dei[1]

Nay, Death, thou art a shadow! Even as light
Is but the shadow of invisible God,
And of that shade the shadow is thin Night,
Veiling the earth whereon our feet have trod;
So art Thou but the shadow of this life,
Itself the pale and unsubstantial shade
Of living God, fulfill'd by love and strife
Throughout the universe Himself hath made:
And as frail Night, following the flight of earth,
Obscures the world we breathe in, for a while,
So Thou, the reflex of our mortal birth,
Veilest the life wherein we weep and smile:
But when both earth and life are whirl'd away,
What shade can shroud us from God's deathless day?

Thomas Hardy (1840–1928)

Transformations

Portion of this yew
Is a man my grandsire knew,
Bosomed here at its foot:
This branch may be his wife,
A ruddy human life
Now turned to a green shoot.

[1] [Light is the shadow of God.]

These grasses must be made
Of her who often prayed,
Last century, for repose;
And the fair girl long ago
Whom I often tried to know
May be entering this rose.

So, they are not underground,
But as nerves and veins abound
In the growths of upper air,
And they feel the sun and rain,
And the energy again
That made them what they were!

The Darkling Thrush

I leant upon a coppice gate
        When Frost was spectre-gray,
And Winter's dregs made desolate
        The weakening eye of day.
The tangled bine-stems scored the sky
        Like strings of broken lyres,
And all mankind that haunted nigh
        Had sought their household fires.

The land's sharp features seem'd to be
        The Century's corpse outleant,
His crypt the cloudy canopy,
        The wind his death-lament.
The ancient pulse of germ and birth
        Was shrunken hard and dry,
And every spirit upon earth
        Seem'd fervourless as I.

At once a voice arose among
        The bleak twigs overhead
In a full-hearted evensong
        Of joy illimited;
An aged thrush, frail, gaunt, and small,
        In blast-beruffled plume,
Had chosen thus to fling his soul
        Upon the growing gloom.

So little cause for carollings
        Of such ecstatic sound

Was written on terrestrial things
    Afar or nigh around,
That I could think there trembled through
    His happy good-night air
Some blèssed Hope, whereof he knew
    And I was unaware.

Gerard Manley Hopkins (1844–1889)

(Carrion Comfort)

Not, I'll not, carrion comfort, Despair, not feast on thee;
Not untwist—slack they may be—these last strands of man
In me ór, most weary, cry *I can no more.* I can;
Can something, hope, wish day come, not choose not to be.
But ah, but O thou terrible, why wouldst thou rude on me
Thy wring-world right foot rock? lay a lionlimb against me? scan
With darksome devouring eyes my bruisèd bones? and fan,
O in turns of tempest, me heaped there; me frantic to avoid thee and flee?

  Why? That my chaff might fly; my grain lie, sheer and clear.
Nay in all that toil, that coil, since (seems) I kissed the rod,
Hand rather, my heart lo! lapped strength, stole joy, would laugh, chéer.
Cheer whom though? the hero whose heaven-handling flung me, fóot tród
Me? or me that fought him? O which one? is it each one? That night, that year
Of now done darkness I wretch lay wrestling with (my God!) my God.

John Banister Tabb (1845–1909)

Evolution

Out of the dusk a shadow,
  Then, a spark;
Out of the cloud a silence,
  Then, a lark;
Out of the heart a rapture,
  Then, a pain;
Out of the dead, cold ashes,
  Life again.

William Ernest Henley (1849–1903)

Invictus

Out of the night that covers me,
   Black as the pit from pole to pole,
I thank whatever gods may be
   For my unconquerable soul.

In the fell clutch of circumstance
   I have not winced nor cried aloud.
Under the bludgeonings of chance
   My head is bloody, but unbowed.

Beyond this place of wrath and tears
   Looms but the Horror of the shade,
And yet the menace of the years
   Finds and shall find me unafraid.

It matters not how strait the gate,
   How charged with punishments the scroll,
I am the master of my fate:
   I am the captain of my soul.

James Whitcomb Riley (1849–1916)

Away

I can not say, and I will not say,
That he is dead—he is just away.
With a cheery smile and a wave of the hand,
He has wandered into an unknown land,
And left us dreaming, how very fair
It needs must be, since he lingers there.
And you—O you, who so wildly yearn
For the old-time step and the glad return,
Think of him faring on, as dear
In the love of There as the love of Here.
Think of him as the same, I say;
He is not dead—he is just away.

Robert Louis Stevenson (1850–1894)

Requiem

Under the wide and starry sky
Dig the grave and let me lie.
Glad did I live and gladly die,
  And I laid me down with a will.

This be the verse you grave for me:
Here he lies where he longed to be;
Home is the sailor, home from sea,
  And the hunter home from the hill.

In Memoriam F. A. S.

Yet, O stricken heart, remember, O remember
  How of human days he lived the better part.
April came to bloom and never dim December
  Breathed its killing chills upon the head or heart.

Doomed to know not winter, only spring, a being
  Trod the flowery April blithely for a while,
Took his fill of music, joy of thought and seeing,
  Came and stayed and went, nor ever ceased to smile.

Came and stayed and went, and now when all is finished,
  You alone have crossed the melancholy stream,
Yours the pang, but his, O his, the undiminished
  Undecaying gladness, undeparted dream.

All that life contains of torture, toil, and treason,
  Shame, dishonor, death, to him were but a name.
Here, a boy, he dwelt through all the singing season
  And ere the day of sorrow departed as he came.

John Davidson (1857–1909)

Song

The boat is chafing at our long delay,
  And we must leave too soon
The spicy sea-pinks and the inborne spray,
  The tawny sands, the moon.

Keep us, O Thetis, in our western flight!
   Watch from thy pearly throne
Our vessel, plunging deeper into night
   To reach a land unknown.

A. E. Housman (1859–1936)

The Night Is Freezing Fast

The night is freezing fast,
   Tomorrow comes December;
      And winterfalls of old
Are with me from the past;
   And chiefly I remember
      How Dick would hate the cold.

Fall, winter, fall; for he,
   Prompt hand and headpiece clever,
      Has woven a winter robe,
And made of earth and sea
   His overcoat for ever,
      And wears the turning globe.

To an Athlete Dying Young

The time you won your town the race
We chaired you through the market-place;
Man and boy stood cheering by,
And home we brought you shoulder-high.

To-day, the road all runners come,
Shoulder-high we bring you home,
And set you at your threshold down,
Townsman of a stiller town.

Smart lad, to slip betimes away
From fields where glory does not stay
And early though the laurel grows
It withers quicker than the rose.

Eyes the shady night has shut
Cannot see the record cut,
And silence sounds no worse than cheers
After earth has stopped the ears:

Now you will not swell the rout
Of lads that wore their honours out,
Runners whom renown outran
And the name died before the man.

So set, before its echoes fade,
The fleet foot on the sill of shade,
And hold to the low lintel up
The still-defended challenge-cup.

And round that early-laurelled head
Will flock to gaze the strengthless dead,
And find unwithered on its curls
The garland briefer than a girl's.

With Rue My Heart Is Laden

With rue my heart is laden
  For golden friends I had,
For many a rose-lipt maiden
  And many a lightfoot lad.

By brooks too broad for leaping
  The lightfoot boys are laid;
The rose-lipt girls are sleeping
  In fields where roses fade.

George Santayana (1863–1952)

To W. P. II

With you a part of me hath passed away;
For in the peopled forest of my mind
A tree made leafless by this wintry wind
Shall never don again its green array.

Chapel and fireside, country road and bay,
Have something of their friendliness resigned;
Another, if I would, I could not find,
And I am grown much older in a day.

But yet I treasure in my memory
Your gift of charity, and young heart's ease,
And the dear honor of your amity;
For these once mine, my life is rich with these.
  And I scarce know which part may greater be,—
  What I keep of you, or you rob from me.

Rudyard Kipling (1865–1936)

The Widower

For a season there must be pain—
For a little, little space
I shall lose the sight of her face,
Take back the old life again
While She is at rest in her place.

For a season this pain must endure,
For a little, little while
I shall sigh more often than smile
Till Time shall work me a cure,
And the pitiful days beguile.

For that season we must be apart,
For a little length of years,
Till my life's last hour nears,
And, above the beat of my heart,
I hear Her voice in my ears.

But I shall not understand—
Being set on some later love,
Shall not know her for whom I strove,
Till she reach me forth her hand,
Saying, "Who but I have the right?"
And out of a troubled night
Shall draw me safe to the land.

Paul Laurence Dunbar (1872–1906)

When All Is Done

When all is done, and my last word is said,
And ye who loved me murmur, "He is dead,"
Let no one weep, for fear that I should know,
And sorrow too that ye should sorrow so.

When all is done and in the oozing clay,
Ye lay this cast-off hull of mine away,
Pray not for me, for, after long despair,
The quiet of the grave will be a prayer.

For I have suffered loss and grievous pain,
The hurts of hatred and the world's disdain,
And wounds so deep that love, well-tried and pure,
Had not the pow'r to ease them or to cure.

When all is done, say not my day is o'er,
And that thro' night I seek a dimmer shore:
Say rather that my morn has just begun,—
I greet the dawn and not a setting sun,
When all is done.

Robert Frost (1874–1963)

Acceptance

When the spent sun throws up its rays on cloud
And goes down burning into the gulf below,
No voice in nature is heard to cry aloud
At what has happened. Birds, at least, must know
It is the change to darkness in the sky.
Murmuring something quiet in her breast,
One bird begins to close a faded eye;
Or overtaken too far from his nest,
Hurrying low above the ground, some waif
Swoops just in time to his remembered tree.
At most he thinks or twitters softly, "Safe!
Now let the night be dark for all of me.
Let the night be too dark for me to see
Into the future. Let what will be, be."

John Masefield (1878–1967)

A Song at Parting

The tick of the blood is settling slow, my heart will soon be still,
And ripe and ready am I for rest in the grave atop the hill;
So gather me up and lay me down, for ready and ripe am I,
For the weary vigil with sightless eyes that may not see the sky.

I have lived my life: I have spilt the wine that God the Maker gave,
So carry me up the lonely hill and lay me in the grave,
And cover me in with cleanly mould and old and lichened stones,
In a place where ever the cry of the wind shall thrill my sleepy bones.

Gather me up and lay me down with an old song and a prayer,
Cover me in with wholesome earth, and weep and leave me there;
And get you gone with a kindly thought and an old tune and a sigh,
And leave me alone, asleep, at rest, for ready and ripe am I.

Edna St. Vincent Millay (1892–1950)

Dirge Without Music

I am not resigned to the shutting away of loving hearts in the hard ground.
So it is, and so it will be, for so it has been, time out of mind:
Into the darkness they go, the wise and the lovely. Crowned
With lilies and with laurel they go; but I am not resigned.

Lovers and thinkers, into the earth with you.
Be one with the dull, the indiscriminate dust.
A fragment of what you felt, of what you knew,
A formula, a phrase remains,—but the best is lost.

The answers quick and keen, the honest look, the laughter, the love,—
They are gone. They are gone to feed the roses. Elegant and curled
Is the blossom. Fragrant is the blossom. I know. But I do not approve.
More precious was the light in your eyes than all the roses in the world.

Down, down, down into the darkness of the grave
Gently they go, the beautiful, the tender,. the kind;
Quietly they go, the intelligent, the witty, the brave.
I know. But I do not approve. And I am not resigned.

W. H. Auden (1907–1973)

Funeral Blues

Stop all the clocks, cut off the telephone,
Prevent the dog from barking with a juicy bone,
Silence the pianos and with muffled drum
Bring out the coffin, let the mourners come.

Let aeroplanes circle moaning overhead
Scribbling on the sky the message He Is Dead.
Put crepe bows round the white necks of public doves,
Let the traffic policemen wear black cotton gloves.

He was my North, my South, my East and West.
My working week and my Sunday rest,
My noon, my midnight, my talk, my song;
I thought that love would last forever; I was wrong.

The stars are not wanted now: put out every one;
Pack up the moon and dismantle the sun;
Pour away the ocean and sweep up the wood;
For nothing now can ever come to any good.

Dylan Thomas (1914–1953)

Do Not Go Gentle into That Good Night

Do not go gentle into that good night,
Old age should burn and rave at close of day;
Rage, rage against the dying of the light.

Though wise men at their end know dark is right,
Because their words had forked no lightning they
Do not go gentle into that good night.

Good men, the last wave by, crying how bright
Their frail deeds might have danced in a green bay,
Rage, rage against the dying of the light.

Wild men who caught and sang the sun in flight,
And learn, too late, they grieved it on its way,
Do not go gentle into that good night.

Grave men, near death, who see with blinding sight
Blind eyes could blaze like meteors and be gay,
Rage, rage against the dying of the light.

And you, my father, there on the sad height,
Curse, bless, me now with your fierce tears, I pray.
Do not go gentle into that good night.
Rage, rage against the dying of the light.

Alphabetical List of Authors, Titles, and First Lines

(Titles are given, in italics, only when distinct from the first lines.)

A *Psalm of Life* 20
A slumber did my spirit seal; 10
Acceptance 50
Adams, Sarah Flowers 18
After great pain, a formal feeling comes: 35
Ah, my Beloved, fill the Cup that clears 22
Akers, Elizabeth 37
Aldrich, James 26
Arnold, Matthew 34
At the last, tenderly, 33
Auden, W. H. 51
Away 45
Because I could not stop for Death, 34
Beddoes, Thomas Lovell 16
Blessed Are They that Mourn 14
Brontë, Emily 29
Browning, Elizabeth Barrett 18
Browning, Robert 27
Bryant, William Cullen 11
Calm on the bosom of thy God, 10
Cardinal Newman, John Henry 16
(Carrion Comfort) 44
Clare, John 11
Close now thine eyes and rest secure; 4
Cold in the earth—and the deep snow piled above thee, 31
Coleridge, Hartley 15
Count each affliction, whether light or grave, 29
Cowper, William 9
Cranch, Christopher 28
Crashaw, Richard 6
Crossing the Bar 23
Darest thou now, O soul, 33
Darkling Thrush, The 43
Davidson, John 46
De Vere, Aubrey Thomas 29
Death 10
Death Be Not Proud 3
Death be not proud, though some have called thee 3
Death stands above me, whispering low 10
Death-Bed, A 26
Death-Bed, The 15
Dickinson, Emily 34
Dirge (Beddoes) 16
Dirge (Hemans) 10
Dirge Without Music 51
Do not go gentle into that good night, 52
Does the road wind up-hill all the way? 35
Donne, John 3
Dunbar, Paul Laurence 49
Dying Christian to His Soul, The 8
Early Death 15
Endurance 37
Enosis 28
Epitaph Upon Husband and Wife, An 6
Eternity 4
Even such is Time, that takes in trust 1
Evolution 44
Farewell, thou child of my right hand, and joy; 3
Fear death?—to feel the fog in my throat, 27
Fear no more the heat o' the sun 2
First Snow-Fall, The 32
FitzGerald, Edward 22

Fly envious Time, till thou run out thy race, 5
For a season there must be pain— 49
Frost, Robert 50
Funeral Blues 51
Garden of Proserpine, The 39
God moves in a mysterious way, 9
Good-Night, A 4
Happy the man, whose wish and care 8
Hardy, Lizzie Clark 41
Hardy, Thomas 42
Hemans, Felicia Dorothea 10
Henley, William Ernest 45
Her suffering ended with the day, 26
Herbert, George 4
Here, where the world is quiet; 39
Herrick, Robert 4
Hood,Thomas 15
Hopkins, Gerard Manley 44
Housman, A. E. 47
How mournful seems, in broken dreams, 21
How much the heart may bear, and yet not break! 37
I Am 11
I am not resigned to the shutting away of loving hearts 51
I am; yet what I am none cares or knows, 11
I can not say, and I will not say, 45
I leant upon a coppice gate 43
I never saw a moor, 35
I strove with none; for none was worth my strife. 10
In Memoriam (selections) 24
In Memoriam F. A. S. 46
Invictus 45
Jonson, Ben 3
King James Bible 1
Kipling, Rudyard 49
Landor, Walter Savage 10
Light Shining Out of Darkness 9
Longfellow, Henry Wadsworth 20
Lowell, James Russell 32
Lux Est Umbra Dei 42
Masefield, John 50
Millay, Edna St. Vincent 51
Milton, John 5
My Mother 27
My soul, there is a country 7
Nay, Death, thou art a shadow! Even as light 42
No coward soul is mine, 29
Norton, Caroline Elizabeth 21
Not Lost, But Gone Before 21
Not, I'll not, carrion comfort, Despair, not feast on thee; 44
O Earth, lie heavily upon her eyes; 37
O years! and Age! Farewell: 4
Ode on Solitude 8
Of all the thoughts of God that are 18
Oh, deem not they are blest alone 14
On My First Son 3
On Time 5
Out of the dusk a shadow, 44
Out of the night that covers me, 45
Peace 7
Peace; come away: the song of woe 24
Poe, Edgar Allan 17
Poor soul, the centre of my sinful earth, 2
Pope, Alexander 8
Portion of this yew 42
Prospice 27
Psalm 23 1
Quarles, Francis 4
Rainy Day, The 20
Raleigh, Walter 1
Remember 36
Remember me when I am gone away, 36
Remembrance 31
Requiem 46
Requiem, A 38
Requiescat 34
Rest (Newman) 17
Rest (Rossetti) 37
Riley, James Whitcomb 45
Rossetti, Christina Georgina 35
Rubaiyat of Omar Khayyám, The (selections) 22
Santayana, George 48
Scott, William Bell 27
Shakespeare, William 2
She died in beauty,—like a rose 19
She passed away like morning dew 15

Sillery, Charles Doyne 19
Sleep, The 18
Some Time at Eve 41
Some time at eve when the tide is low, 41
Song 46
Song at Parting, A 50
Sorrow 29
Sorrow, lie still and wear 16
Stevenson, Robert Louis 46
Stop all the clocks, cut off the telephone, 51
Strew on her roses, roses, 34
Sunset and evening star, 23
Sweet day, so cool, so calm, so bright! 4
Swinburne, Algernon Charles 39
Symonds, John Addington 42
Sympathy 30
Tabb, John Banister 44
Tell me not, in mournful numbers, 20
Tennyson, Alfred Lord 23
Thanatopsis 11
The boat is chafing at our long delay, 46
The day is cold, and dark, and dreary; 20
The Lord is my shepherd; I shall not want. 1
The mourners came at break of day 18
The night is freezing fast, 47
The snow had begun in the gloaming, 32
The tick of the blood is settling slow, 50
The time you won your town the race 47
There should be no despair for you 30
There was a gather'd stillness in the room: 27
They are all gone into the world of light! 6
They are at rest. 16
Thomas, Dylan 52
Thomson, James 38
Thou blossom bright with autumn dew, 13
Thou hast lived in pain and woe, 38
Thou wast all that to me, love, 17
Thought is deeper than all speech, 28
To an Athlete Dying Young 47
To him who in the love of Nature holds 11
To One in Paradise 17
To the Fringed Gentian 13
To these whom death again did wed 6
To W. P. II 48
Transformations 42
Under the wide and starry sky 46
Up-Hill 35
Vaughan, Henry 6
Virtue 4
Vital spark of heavenly flame, 8
We watched her breathing through the night, 15
When all is done, and my last word is said, 49
When I am dead, my dearest, 36
When the spent sun throws up its rays on cloud 50
With you a part of me hath passed away; 48
Whitman, Walt 33
Widower, The 49
With rue my heart is laden 48
Wordsworth, William 10
Yet, O stricken heart, remember, O remember 46